DETECTING EARTHQUAKES

by Marne Ventura

FOCUS
READERS

WWW.NORTHSTAREDITIONS.COM

Produced for North Star Editions by Red Line Editorial.

Photographs ©: Suttisak Soralump/Shutterstock Images, cover, 1; RHG/Shutterstock Images, 4–5; Niranjan Shrestha/AP Images, 7; Dutourdumonde Photography/Shutterstock Images, 9; Fotos593/Shutterstock Images, 10–11; Johan Swanepoel/iStockphoto/Thinkstock, 13; AP Images, 15; Dorling Kindersley/Thinkstock, 16–17; Kyodo/Newscom, 18–19; SSPL/Getty Images, 21; Jes Aznar/AFP/Getty Images, 22; Inga Spence/Science Source, 24–25; Jessica Wilson/NASA/Science Source, 27

Content Consultant: Professor John Ebel, Department of Earth and Environmental Sciences, Boston College

ISBN
978-1-63517-001-6 (hardcover)
978-1-63517-057-3 (paperback)
978-1-63517-163-1 (ebook pdf)
978-1-63517-113-6 (hosted ebook)

Library of Congress Control Number: 2016949784

Printed in the United States of America
Mankato, MN
November, 2016

ABOUT THE AUTHOR

Marne Ventura is the author of 41 books for kids. She loves writing about nature, science, technology, food, health, and crafts. She is a former elementary school teacher and holds a master's degree in education from the University of California. Marne lives with her husband on the central coast of California, west of the San Andreas Fault.

TABLE OF CONTENTS

CHAPTER 1

EARTHQUAKE!

Rasmila Awal hurried down the busy street in Kathmandu, Nepal. Her five-month-old son, Sonies, and ten-year-old daughter, Soniya, were at home. The baby was sleeping. Mrs. Awal knew she could count on her daughter to watch him for a few minutes. Her husband, a bus driver, was at work.

Kathmandu is a beautiful city located near tall mountains.

Suddenly Mrs. Awal heard a rumble. Buildings shook, dropping bricks and broken windows onto the street. People screamed and ran in all directions. Mrs. Awal's heart pounded. She raced for home. As she rounded the corner, she saw her building collapse into **rubble**.

The ground continued to rumble as Mrs. Awal ran to the place where her door had been. She called out for help. Her eyes filled with tears. She knelt down to pull away broken pieces of the building.

Soon Mr. Awal joined his wife. Soldiers from the Nepalese army came to help. There was good news after a couple of hours. Soniya was found unhurt.

The earthquake quickly reduced many of the city's buildings to rubble.

But where was baby Sonies? It was getting dark. The rescue workers couldn't see. The search would have to wait for morning.

The minute the sun rose, the Awals returned to the search site. Soon they heard a baby crying. The soldiers lifted away **debris**. It was Sonies! Aside from a bruise on his face and a cut on his thigh, he was unharmed.

The earthquake that destroyed the Awals' home shook Nepal on April 25, 2015. More than 5,500 people died,

EARTHQUAKE RESCUES

Disaster response teams must act quickly to save people buried in the rubble after an earthquake. Rescue dogs use their sensitive sense of smell to find survivors. Workers lower tiny video cameras into collapsed buildings to see if anyone is inside.

Rescuers searched through the debris for survivors after the Nepal earthquake.

and more than twice that number were hurt. The earthquake had struck without warning. **Seismologists** do not yet know how to predict when a quake will happen.

However, experts have made major advances in detecting and measuring quakes. Their work has saved many lives.

CHAPTER 2

THE SCIENCE BEHIND EARTHQUAKES

Earthquakes happen every day, all over the planet. Most are not as bad as the one in Nepal. But when a strong earthquake hits, it can cause severe damage. One of the earliest records of a powerful quake dates back to more than 3,000 years ago in ancient China.

Earthquakes can severely damage the ground and anything standing on it.

In modern times, scientists have made big breakthroughs in detecting earthquakes.

Earth is made up of three major layers. The crust covers the surface of the planet. It averages approximately 20 miles (32 km) thick on land. Under the ocean, the crust is approximately 3 miles (4.8 km) thick on average.

Below the crust is a layer called the mantle. This layer is approximately 1,800 miles (2,900 km) thick. The mantle is made of hot rock.

Earth's center is the core. It has an inner part and an outer part. It is made of both solid and liquid metal—mostly iron.

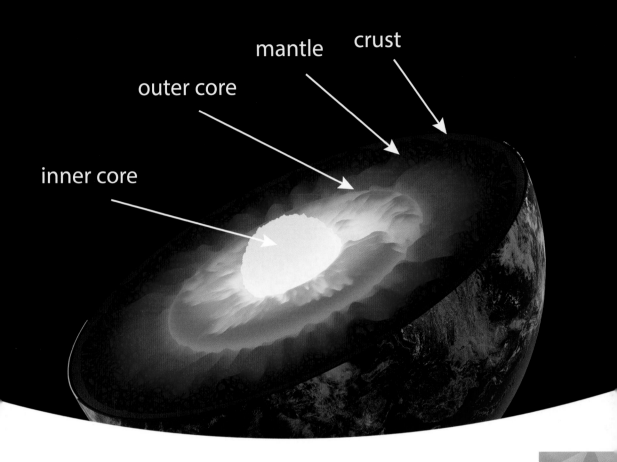

inner core

outer core

mantle

crust

Earth's inner layers are very hot.

Earth's crust is divided into pieces called plates. These plates rest on top of the mantle. They are always moving and shifting on the mantle. The place where two plates meet is called a fault. This is a spot where an earthquake can begin.

Some plates simply slide past each other at the fault. Other plates slide away from each other. Sometimes plates bump into each other and get stuck. Energy builds up as one plate pushes against the other. The rocks compress. Finally, the plates slip past each other. The energy from the compressed rock is released and moves out in waves. This is an earthquake.

Early one morning in 1906, a terrible earthquake shook the city of San Francisco, California. More than 3,000 people died. Scientists at the time knew little about earthquakes.

Soon after the quake, a team of **geologists** showed that a fault 800 miles

The 1906 earthquake caused fires that raged through San Francisco.

(1,300 km) long divides two plates in California. Movement at this fault, called the San Andreas Fault, caused the earthquake. This was a big breakthrough in earthquake science.

EARTH'S PLATES

In 1912, Alfred Wegener came up with the idea that Earth once had a single continent surrounded by a vast ocean. Over many years, the continent divided and huge plates slowly drifted apart.

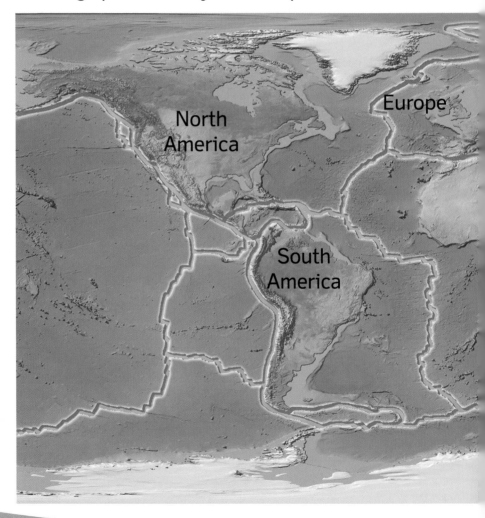

Later in the 1900s, scientists identified these plates. Earthquakes are most common along the faults between them. This map shows Earth's major faults.

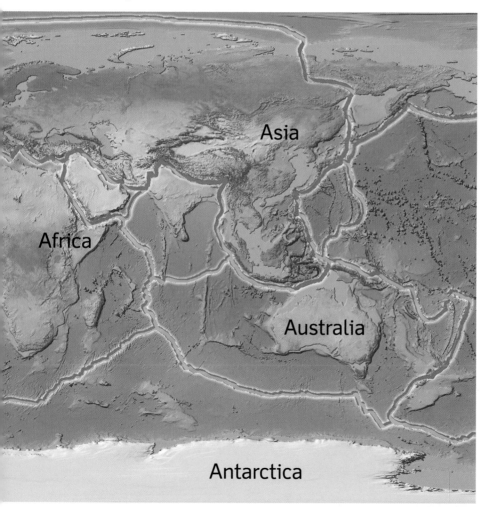

CHAPTER 3

MEASURING EARTHQUAKES

When plates suddenly slip past one another, they release energy in the form of seismic waves. These invisible waves begin deep within the planet.

Scientists measure seismic waves with a seismograph. Inside this device, the movement of the ground causes a **pendulum** to swing back and forth.

A scientist sets up a seismograph in Japan.

A magnetic field surrounds the pendulum, creating an electric current when the pendulum moves. Seismologists use the changes in this electric current to determine the strength of the shaking.

EARLY EARTHQUAKE DETECTION

In China in 132 CE, Zhang Heng made the first known earthquake detector. It was a large jar with eight dragon heads facing outward. Openmouthed ceramic toads sat below the dragon heads. The dragons held balls in their mouths. When the ground shook, a pendulum moved inside the jar. It caused a ball to drop from a dragon's mouth into a toad's mouth. If the toad was on the east side, Zhang knew the source of the earthquake was to the east.

Zhang Heng's device was one early method of detecting earthquakes.

The seismograph records over a long period of time, so scientists can also see how long the earthquake lasted. By comparing the times that seismic waves arrive at different locations, scientists can determine where the earthquake started.

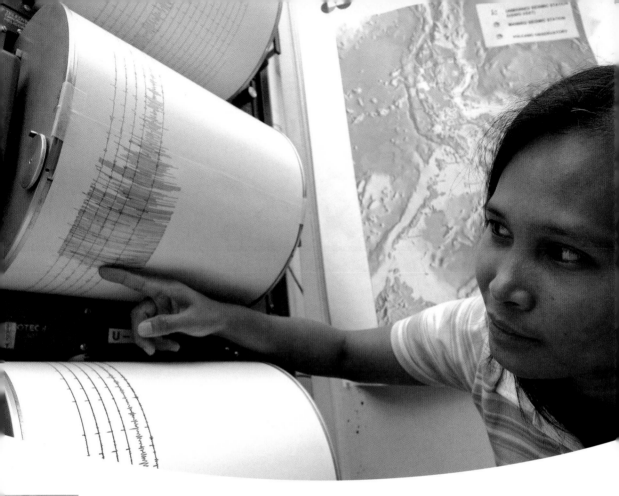

A scientist studies the data from a seismograph in the Philippines.

Scientists use several ways to rate the power of earthquakes. They include the moment magnitude scale and the Mercalli scale. The moment magnitude scale measures the seismic energy of an earthquake at its source. Earthquake moment magnitudes generally range between 0 and 10. Earthquakes with a magnitude of 6.0 or higher are considered major quakes.

The Mercalli scale is a rating of the intensity of an earthquake's shaking. It is given in Roman numerals, and it ranges from I to XII, or 1 to 12. Intensity is how strong the shaking is felt on Earth's surface. Scientists assign a Mercalli scale number based on the shaking people feel or the damage they observe.

CHAPTER 4

PREVENTING DAMAGE AND BEING PREPARED

Seismologists all over the world now monitor earthquake activity. They report where quakes happen. From these reports, seismologists have learned that most earthquakes occur in a zone called the Ring of Fire. This horseshoe-shaped area runs along faults around the edges of the Pacific Ocean.

Monitoring stations transmit seismograph data to scientists for study.

New technology may help scientists monitor earthquake activity in the future. Advanced computers record and analyze data faster and better. Measuring devices are buried in faults to measure movement and pressure. Scientists are also working on new ways to use **satellites** for earthquake detection. The satellites can sense how the shaking of the earthquake causes vibrations in the atmosphere.

Even without earthquake prediction, there are many ways to help people stay safe. **Engineers** can make old buildings and bridges stronger to help them survive quakes. This process is called retrofitting.

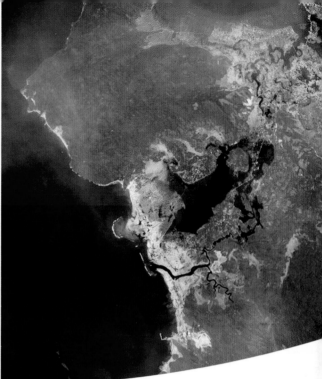

A satellite view shows Aceh, Indonesia, before (left) and after (right) a 2004 earthquake.

After the Great East Japan earthquake in 2011, scientists began work on a high-rise building with an earthquake **sensor** to detect damage. This could give people time to escape if the building might be at risk of collapsing.

The research of seismologists has improved our understanding of earthquakes. These scientists have discovered where earthquakes are most likely to occur. They take steps to protect people in these areas. The study of these devastating disasters has saved many lives.

RETROFITTING

The process of retrofitting makes old buildings safer in the event of an earthquake. Workers may add bolts to connect a structure more tightly to its foundation. They may add braces to stiffen a building's walls. These changes can help prevent a building from collapsing.

EARTHQUAKE SAFETY CHECKLIST

- Identify safe places to take shelter in your home, such as under sturdy pieces of furniture.

- Make sure there are no loose items that could fall and hurt people if an earthquake happens.

- Have an earthquake kit ready. It should include bottled water, food, a flashlight, and a first aid kit.

- Make an earthquake plan with your family, and figure out a safe place to meet with them.

- During an earthquake, drop to the ground so the earthquake doesn't knock you off your feet.

- Cover your head and neck with your arms to protect against falling items.

- After the shaking stops, find a clear path to safety, exit the building, and move to an open space.

- If you are outside when an earthquake hits, move away from buildings, streetlights, and telephone poles.

- If an earthquake happens, avoid any broken pipes or fallen power lines.

FOCUS ON
DETECTING
EARTHQUAKES

Write your answers on a separate piece of paper.

1. Summarize Chapter 2 of this book.

2. If scientists one day discover how to predict earthquakes, how would that change earthquake safety? What new steps could people take to protect themselves?

3. What is the center of Earth called?

    A. the crust
    B. the mantle
    C. the core

4. What can be measured with a seismograph?

    A. the moment magnitude scale rating of an earthquake
    B. the Mercalli scale rating of an earthquake
    C. the time and location of an upcoming earthquake

Answer key on page 32.

GLOSSARY

debris
The remains of something broken.

engineers
People who design buildings or structures.

geologists
Scientists who study Earth's crust.

pendulum
An object suspended from a rod or string that swings freely.

rubble
Broken stones or bricks from a building.

satellites
Devices that orbit Earth.

seismologists
Scientists who study earthquakes and earthquake waves.

sensor
A device that detects things, such as movement.

TO LEARN MORE

BOOKS

Burgan, Michael. *Surviving Earthquakes.* Chicago: Raintree, 2012.

Suen, Anastasia. *Earthquakes.* Vero Beach, FL: Rourke, 2016.

Ventura, Marne. *How to Survive an Earthquake.* Mankato, MN: The Child's World, 2015.

NOTE TO EDUCATORS

Visit **www.focusreaders.com** to find lesson plans, activities, links, and other resources related to this title.

INDEX

Answer Key: 1. Answers will vary; **2.** Answers will vary; **3.** C; **4.** A